LEARN TO DRAW ANGRY BIRDS™
BAD PiGGiES™

Walter Foster Jr.

ROVIO BOOKS

This library edition published in 2015 by Walter Foster Jr.,
an imprint of Quarto Publishing Group USA Inc.
3 Wrigley, Suite A
Irvine, CA 92618

Step-by-step illustrations by Kristina Burr
© 2009–2014 Rovio Entertainment Ltd.

Distributed in the United States and Canada by
Lerner Publisher Services
241 First Avenue North
Minneapolis, MN 55401 U.S.A.
www.lernerbooks.com

First Library Edition

Library of Congress Cataloging-in-Publication Data

Learn to draw Angry Birds Bad Piggies / step-by-step illustrations by Kristina Burr. -- First Library Edition.
    pages cm
  ISBN 978-1-939581-46-4
1. Bad Piggies (Fictitious characters)--Juvenile literature. 2. Drawing--Technique--Juvenile literature.
I. Marroquin-Burr, Kristina, illustrator.
  NC1764.8.B33L43 2015
  741.5'1--dc23

                                                              2014026668

062015
18882

9 8 7 6 5 4 3 2 1

TABLE OF CONTENTS

MEET THE BAD PIGGIES

Angry Birds versus the Bad Piggies has become an epic conflict, which has gained billions of supporters on both sides. But have you ever heard the Piggies' side of the story?

The pigs are much more than the green villains of the Angry Birds—they are generally bright-eyed and fun-loving creatures. They love to talk, and a simple "OINK!" punctuates most of their sentences. Even though they crash and burn a lot, they are always playful and optimistic, "keeping it squeal" and going from one adventure to the next "on a pig and a prayer." The pigs are crafty and creative, but also have a silly side, as they are often "snout and about" having fun. In the world of the Bad Piggies, it's "bright lights, Pig City."

Now the pigs' latest mission is to reconstruct their map, which has been scattered all over Piggy Island. King Pig has ordered his loyal minions to find and steal the eggs—the pigs are inventive problem solvers. Armed with an assortment of ever-changing items, their task is to construct vehicles that will recover the eggs, but sometimes their designs end up crashing and exploding along the way. The Piggies do their best to fulfill their mission with the most imaginative and fun vehicles, even if it means breaking some bones! Turn the page for a peek inside the Bad Piggies' plans...

The pigs watch intently as the Angry Birds slumber peacefully alongside their eggs.

King Pig sends one slightly nervous Minion Pig as a spy.
Once he returns, King Pig has a brilliant idea for how to steal the eggs.

The pigs hurry back to their campsite for one very important tool—the telescope!

Finally they have a perfect view of the eggs. Now it's time to devise a plan.
Mechanic Pig gets to work creating a map, while King Pig daydreams on his throne,
drooling over the thought of eating the delicious eggs. Meanwhile, Minion Pig
becomes curious about the unknown red button on the fan. He decides to press it, and...

OOPS! The blast of air that shoots from the fan tears Mechanic Pig's map into pieces, and the Piggies watch in total dismay as it flies across the beach.

Frightened, Minion Pig hurriedly pieces the map back together. Where could that "X" be leading to? King Pig is furious, convinced the eggs are lost for good, when suddenly Mechanic Pig spots the telescope on a nearby rock!

Look—it's the eggs!!

Everybody becomes frantic in their excitement. Mechanic Pig immediately begins to draw a new map, but King Pig demands to move on to a more, er, powerful strategy.

Minion Pig thinks this sounds like a good idea and decides to take matters into his own hands. He carefully loads a box with explosives, marking it with a clear route to the eggs, when...

Uh-oh...King Pig is NOT happy. Looks like the Piggies' mission is right back where it started.

TOOLS & MATERIALS

Before you begin drawing, you need to gather the right tools. Start with a regular pencil, an eraser, and a pencil sharpener. When you're finished with your drawing, you can bring your characters to life by adding color with crayons, colored pencils, markers, or even paint!

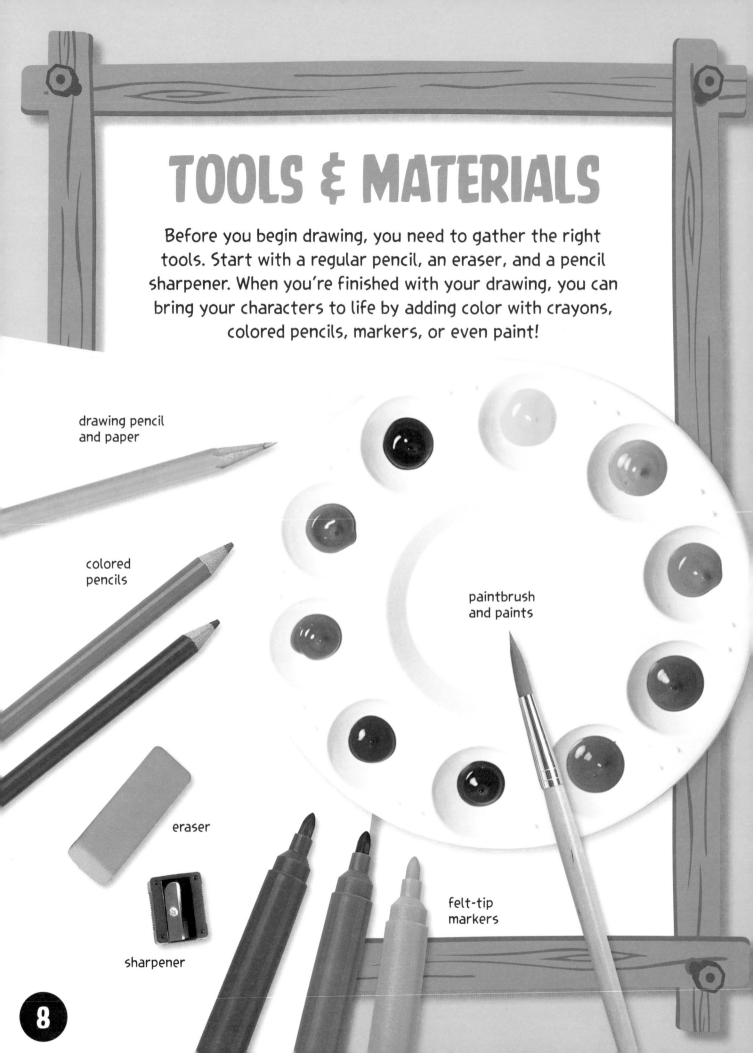

drawing pencil and paper

colored pencils

paintbrush and paints

eraser

sharpener

felt-tip markers

HOW TO USE THIS BOOK

Professional artists draw characters in steps. The key is to start with simple shapes and gradually add the details. The blue lines will help guide you through the process.

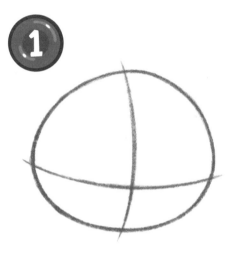

First you'll draw guidelines to help position the character's features.

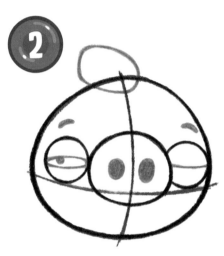

Next you'll add the details step by step.

When you finish adding the details, erase your guidelines. Then darken your final sketch lines with a pen or a marker.

SIZE CHART

Mechanic Pig

Professor Pig

Minion Pig

Corporal Pig

Chronicler Pig

Chef Pig

Foreman Pig

King Pig

MINION PIGS

Minion Pigs are a quirky, kind-hearted bunch. They're always having fun, especially when Corporal Pig and King Pig aren't looking! These guys often snicker at their superiors when they aren't around. As a whole, the Minion Pigs don't actually hate the Angry Birds. They are only after the eggs because that's what King Pig wants them to do.

OINK!

To draw a relieved Minion Pig, follow the same beginning steps from the previous page!

TNT

TNT

OINK!

To draw a damaged Minion Pig, follow the same beginning steps from pages 12-13!

MINION PIGS' EXPRESSIONS

DAMAGED

BLINKING

SCARED

LAUGHING

SAD

TONGUE OUT

SLEEPY

RELIEVED

19

MECHANIC PIG

Similar in size to the Minion Pigs, the Mechanic Pig's blue engineer cap is his trademark accessory. Mechanic Pig is responsible for the devices and materials that make up the pigs' contraptions. He sifts through any debris that finds its way to the island, and he is able to fix machines in a way no other pig can. When there's a problem, every pig on the island knows Mechanic Pig will fix it!

1

25

MECHANIC PIG'S EXPRESSIONS

DAMAGED

LAUGHING

SCARED

SAD

TONGUE OUT

SLEEPY

CORPORAL PIG

Although he is the leader of King Pig's army, Corporal Pig's helmet is the only feature distinguishing his rank. Collateral damage and casualties are not his concern, and unfortunately he's not very smart. Schemes he is in charge of often end in total disaster, and he is only able to command four minions at a time without becoming distressed!

29

He

CORPORAL PIG'S EXPRESSIONS

DAMAGED

LAUGHING

SCARED

SAD

TONGUE OUT

SLEEPY

FOREMAN PIG

Foreman Pig is chief of the Minion Pigs. He ranks above Corporal Pig and is almost as large as King Pig, but sits just below him in the pig hierarchy. Foreman Pig sports a bright orange moustache and matching eyebrows.

FOREMAN PIG'S EXPRESSIONS

DAMAGED

LAUGHING

SCARED

SAD

TONGUE OUT

SLEEPY

KING PIG

Also known as "Smooth Cheeks," King Pig is the biggest pig, making him the leader! He's so lazy that Minion Pigs have to carry him around in his chair. All he really does is throw temper tantrums—other pigs even have to administer punishment on his behalf! Although King Pig has ordered the Minion Pigs to steal the Angry Birds' eggs, rumor has it he has never actually eaten any eggs—a fact that, if found out, would destroy any legitimacy he might have.

KING PIG'S EXPRESSIONS

DAMAGED

BLINKING

SCARED

RELIEVED

TONGUE OUT

SLEEPY

CHEF PIG

The most intelligent of the pigs, Chef Pig is always scheming to eat the eggs himself and become king. Chef Pig is known for being a bit snobbish and paranoid.

1

CHEF PIG'S EXPRESSIONS

DAMAGED

LAUGHING

SCARED

ANGRY

ANNOYED

SCHEMING

PROFESSOR PIG

Honest, pacifist Professor Pig comes up with brilliant, peaceful inventions. Unfortunately, the rest of the pigs somehow always find a way to turn his careful designs into dangerous machines!

CHRONICLER PIG

As the oldest pig, Chronicler Pig knows the history and laws of pig society. Unfortunately, he is becoming absent-minded in his old age and, at times, can be a bit pompous!

KING PIG ON HIS THRONE

King Pig can usually be found sitting on his throne, wearing a shiny golden crown adorned with bright blue sapphires. One or more Minion Pigs are never far behind—awaiting whatever silly command they might receive next!

BUILDING TOOLS

The Bad Piggies rely on all kinds of handy tools and gadgets to build their contraptions. Learn how to create a Bad Piggies-approved vehicle using parts like balloons, parachutes, propellers, and wheels. You can refer to the machines shown on the next few pages as inspiration to create your own original designs! Remember, Mechanic Pig is ready to offer his assistance if you need help. Be creative, and have fun!

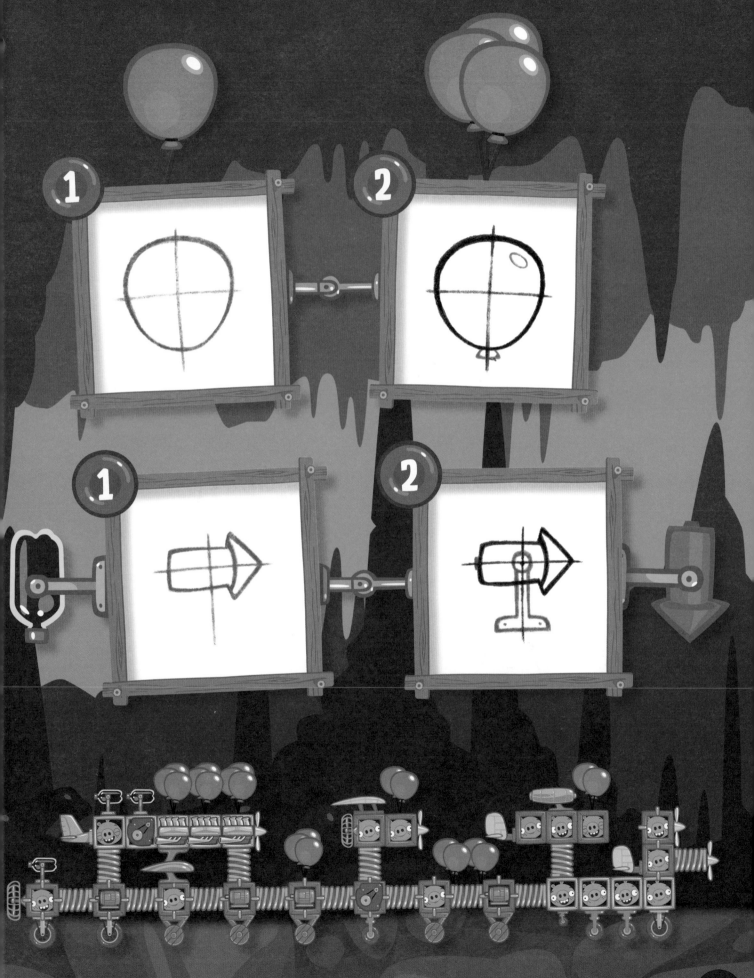

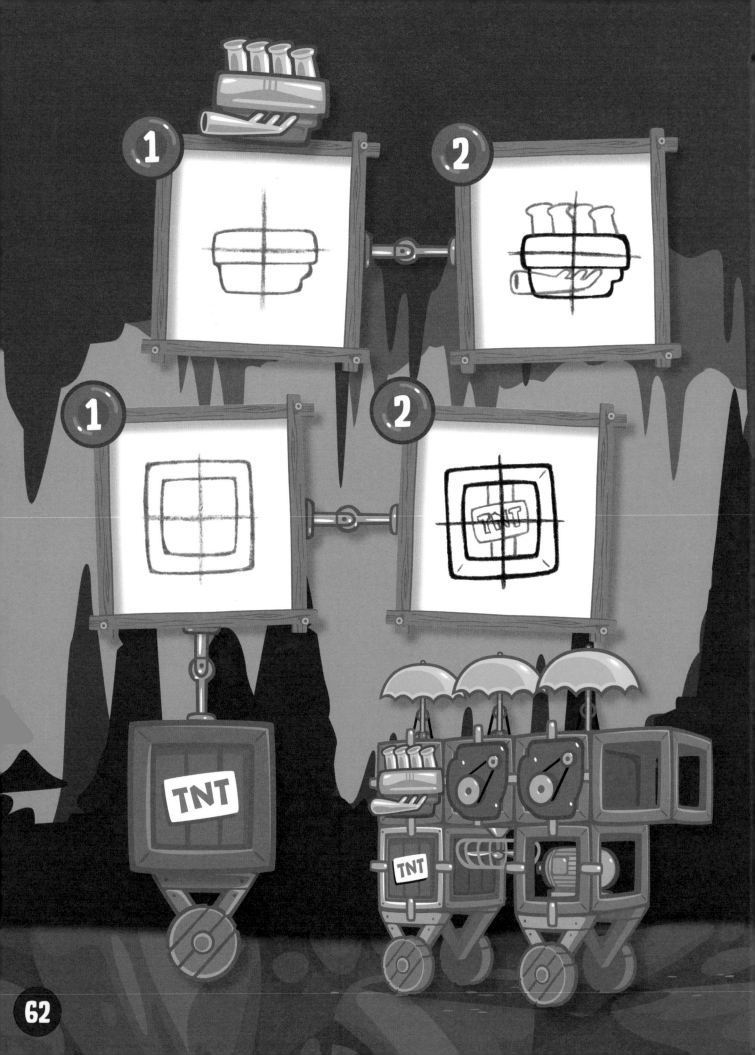

THE END

Now that you've visited Piggy Island and have learned all about the Bad Piggies, you can practice all kinds of crafty, creative adventures on your own! All you need is a pencil, paper, and your imagination!